I AM CXO, NOW WHAT?

A JOB DESCRIPTION FOR LIVING A LIFE OF PURPOSE AND MEANING

DAN BURNETT

WESTBOW PRESS®
A DIVISION OF THOMAS NELSON
& ZONDERVAN

Copyright © 2017 Dan Burnett.

Foreword by Dr. Kathie Amidei

All rights reserved. No part of this book may be used or reproduced by any means, graphic, electronic, or mechanical, including photocopying, recording, taping or by any information storage retrieval system without the written permission of the author except in the case of brief quotations embodied in critical articles and reviews.

All scriptures taken from the New American Bible (Revised Edition).

Scripture quotations taken from the New American Standard Bible® (NASB), Copyright © 1960, 1962, 1963, 1968, 1971, 1972, 1973, 1975, 1977, 1995 by The Lockman Foundation.Used by permission. www.Lockman.org

WestBow Press books may be ordered through booksellers or by contacting:

WestBow Press
A Division of Thomas Nelson & Zondervan
1663 Liberty Drive
Bloomington, IN 47403
www.westbowpress.com
1 (866) 928-1240

Because of the dynamic nature of the Internet, any web addresses or links contained in this book may have changed since publication and may no longer be valid. The views expressed in this work are solely those of the author and do not necessarily reflect the views of the publisher, and the publisher hereby disclaims any responsibility for them.

Any people depicted in stock imagery provided by Thinkstock are models, and such images are being used for illustrative purposes only.
Certain stock imagery © Thinkstock.

ISBN: 978-1-5127-7942-4 (sc)
ISBN: 978-1-5127-7943-1 (hc)
ISBN: 978-1-5127-7941-7 (e)

Library of Congress Control Number: 2017904152

Print information available on the last page.

WestBow Press rev. date: 03/27/2017

DEDICATION

In loving memory of Dad, the first and greatest CXO I encountered. Thank you, Mom for providing me the single greatest "Hallmark moment;" it continues to inspire and calibrate me to this day. To my wife, Denise, for being my biggest advocate and best friend; you make me want to be a better CXO every day. To my children—my greatest source of pride, I hope you grow to love yourself and others as God loves you; created perfectly in His image. And to all my friends who help me see the CXO inside me; you know who you are and, if not, I have more work to do.

TABLE OF CONTENTS

Foreword ix

About the book xiii

Preface xv

Introduction xix

1 Being Best 1

2 The Caption 17

3 Do Good 25

4 I can do this 29

5 Wait, can I do this? 47

6 The heart of the matter 53

7 Will it hurt? 69

8 What are you waiting for? 73

Appendix 79

About the Author 85

FOREWORD

One of the roles that I consider most important in my ministry is facilitating parent sessions for a Family Faith Formation Program, which has been the subject of my life's work. In over twenty years this program has involved hundreds of families and thousands of parents. A few years ago, one dad got my attention when he approached me at the end of the year with a suggestion about a direction I might take in the following year's programming. Not only was this the first dad to offer such an opinion he was also the first parent to indicate how seriously he was taking this program and how closely he was analyzing the experience. My first thought was, "Who is this guy? Either this program is far more impactful than I thought or this is a unique man!" Over time, I have come to believe the latter is the truth.

That man was Dan Burnett, author of this book. This brief exchange began a relationship I have come to appreciate as a blessing and a gift in my life. Over the years our conversations have been both intentional and far-reaching in nature. Through them I have come to know, deeply respect, and love Dan as well as treasure his family. Dan and his family are the kind of people that imperceptibly yet impressively enrich a faith community.

I believe my second encounter with Dan was as one of the guests at Dan and his wife, Denise's "Gratitude Dinner" that you will read about in this book. My first encounter had alerted me that Dan was a thoughtful man; that he was someone who thinks deeply about life. He was someone whose philosophy of life was to "pay attention," a practice of many spiritual guides and leaders. The concept of the "Gratitude Dinner" helped me to see Dan's thoughtfulness had another meaning. He was thoughtful in the sense of being a caring, kind, altruistic, and generous person.

Having the privilege of previewing and observing the evolution of this book and now reading the final copy has led me to a third understanding of Dan's thoughtfulness, that of being a person who is contemplative, pondering in a profound way, the essence of life itself and its meaning.

If there is a more central question of life than our response to that of our personal meaning and purpose I don't know what it is. Dan has taken that question head on. He describes in an accessible, pure, and comprehensible way how to become a CXO, a Chief Experience Officer, and goes on to convince us this is nothing short of the most important role we will ever take on for our family, friends and co-workers. Dan makes a clear, concise case for taking the job description seriously to live a more meaningful and purpose driven life.

I found exceptional insight in his notion that our values are our boss. Having been a religious educator for decades I found he captured the value of living by a moral code in such a way that many would find helpful, and would be compatible with most religious traditions. He offers a very practical guide to moral decision making, a topic that can be complicated and difficult to integrate into everyday life.

Recently I have stood with several suffering friends struggling with loss, depression, having loved ones in the grips of addiction and other things no one would wish for anyone. I have ached for them and wept with my inability to help them. And recently I have also soared with unmitigated gratefulness to know that my simple presence to one of my crying grandchildren is next to magical. But life most often falls in between the helpless empathy

I felt with my suffering friends and the clarity of purpose of simply being there for a child. That is when having a job description for a meaningful life comes in quite handy.

In a life, full of to-do lists it can be difficult to prioritize and embrace the responsibility to be… to be beloved… to be God's child… to be wife, husband, father, mother, brother, sister, son, daughter, friend. The spiritual writer, Henri Nouwen said this sense of belovedness leaps over the questions of what we have accomplished, what we own or what anyone thinks of us. It is to have the lens of knowing our meaning and purpose in our most true "jobs," that of being a human being, God's precious child.

This is a book about faith and life. These are not usually topics that are articulated with a simple elegance but I am not surprised Dan has accomplished this. As with knowing Dan, in reading this book, I am consistently moved by his authenticity, the depth of his heart, and the intentional way he is a husband, a dad, a son, a friend. Dan is solid as a rock, deep as a theologian, and genuine to his core. He is now sharing on the printed page a guide for life and love. This is a book to take to heart.

-Dr. Kathie Amidei

ABOUT THE BOOK

I Am CXO, Now What? is the apex of Dan Burnett's journey from the child of a grocer to a meandering teen, unaware young adult, maturing man, and eventually a self-actualizing Christian. Dan believes we are all called to be better people, and we should take ownership over our experiences with others. Being the chief officer in charge of other peoples' encounters with you requires a simple yet profound set of guidelines. Dan presents the expectations and requirements of the role in the form of a job description—one that will lead you to a life of purpose and meaning.

PREFACE

> Be eager to present yourself as acceptable to
> God, a workman who causes no disgrace,
> imparting the word of truth without deviation.
>
> 2 Timothy 2:15

I have spent most of my life in the education field. Forever a student and lifelong learner with twenty years of experience as an adult educator, I am enamored by connections in learning. I find joy when learners connect with one another, connect with the subject of the learning, and connect with the "teacher." Connections are deeply at the core of what life is all about—emotional, psychological, interpersonal, meta-cognitive, and spiritual connections.

Most of my work has come in the form of workplace learning and performance. I have spent my career training employees on soft and hard-skills to help them make connections and be more effective on the job. I also serve as a catechist in my church helping youth and adults embark on a completely different path of discovery—connecting with their Faith. In all cases, never have I seen learners make connections—feel inspired and eager to apply what they learned—as when I talk about adding purpose and meaning to their life. People are often instructed on what to DO; whether it is a computer program, math equation, or leadership principle. I find people are yearning for support and guidance on simply how to BE.

I am a more confident orator than writer and until recently never had the ambition to be an author. I believe my greatest gift is my ability to connect with people through the charism of public speaking. But I had a message in my heart and needed to leverage any opportunity to share it. Before deciding to write this book, I talked about the concept of a CXO to family, trusted advisors, and professional association groups. The response overwhelmed me. Everyone connected with the basic tenets of a CXO in a manner relevant to them. I learned people need to be reminded from time to time there is a better way. It was that response, and a lot of prayer and discernment, that prompted me to write this book. Helping others sort through the clutter to connect with a better route for becoming the best person they can be satisfies my spiritual desires.

I want you to be comforted, inspired, and joyful. I want you to learn about yourself and embrace deep reflection. I want you to live with intentionality and not merely go through the motions. And I want you to love openly, starting with yourself. I want you to connect with people to live a life of purpose and meaning. Most notably, I want to support you in learning how to BE. Life is an endless journey of discovery and I am with you all the way.

INTRODUCTION

> Just so, your light must shine before others, that they may see your good deeds and glorify your heavenly Father. Matthew 5:16

"What's in a name? That which we call a rose by any other name would smell as sweet." In this classic line from Shakespeare's *Romeo and Juliet*, Juliet is saying a name is artificial and meaningless. She loves Romeo the person, not his Montague family name or anything that comes with it. After all, what's in a name?

What's in a title? Like in Juliet's example, the person is more important than his or her title. Yet I have long pondered what it would be like to have a title that made me part of the C-suite. You know them—the collective group of most important senior executives in an organization whose titles all start with the letter

C, for Chief. In 1987 I was fifteen years old and the movies *Wall Street* and *The Secret to My Success* hit the big screen. I loved them both. I imagined myself in the high-profile, fast-paced, big money executive wing. I concede in both movies the main characters didn't achieve their status the right way, but I was young and didn't appreciate the values of honesty and integrity like I do today; but more on that later. Fast forward to 2017 and look at the employee directory of any of today's modern organizations and you are likely to find titles like CEO, COO, CFO, CIO, CMO, CCO, CLO, and more out there. It is a veritable bowl of C-level alphabet soup.

While doing research for my role in leadership development, I read an article about an organization that introduced a CXO position; which stood for Chief Customer Experience Officer. Customers are certainly as important as Information Technology, Finance, Compliance, or Operations. Why not a CXO to signify customer experience as a major differentiator of competitors? The CXO position sends a message saying the company is serious about having its products and services fully driven by the needs of the customers. But what's in a title? As the saying goes, "actions speak louder than words."

This got me thinking about the quality of experiences I provide and the people who I could view as my own "customers;" specifically co-workers, friends, family, and any other random person I interact with on a day-to-day basis. I concluded that I am a driving factor in their human experience. Let me repeat myself. I am a driving factor that determines the merit of someone else's human experience. More than any name or title could give that is what it means to have influence. I can affect morale, engagement, loyalty, and behavior. I can transform culture. I can make people and intrinsic human needs more important than numbers, processes, or my own priorities. I can create a human experience that makes the people I interact with want to run and tell ten other people about it. I have complete and total autonomy over this wildly exciting opportunity. And all it takes are relatively easy and inexpensive actions I will detail in this book.

I am a CXO, but what's in a title? While I may not officially hold a C-level position or corner office with a view, I am in charge of human experiences. I am the CXO for my family, friends, co-workers, and acquaintances. To remind me of the responsibility, I wrote the letters C-X-O on a cup that I regularly drink from throughout the day. Every time I look at it I am reminded of how

I aspire to conduct myself. I am reminded to strive to be the best person I can be. I am created perfectly and purposefully in God's image to be no one else but me.

Self-help writer and leadership speaker Robin Sharma is credited with saying, "Success is not a function of the size of your title but the richness of your contribution." I would add to that, the relationship between the size of the title and the significance of the contribution is inversely proportional; in other words, the smaller the title the more impactful the contribution. The two best examples I can give you are, "Mom" and "Dad." In my opinion, there are no greater names on earth that you could be called. But what's in a name?

To be the best mom, dad, sibling, friend, employee, volunteer, and person you can be, I recommend you try being a CXO—Chief Experience Officer. CXO is a short title with a big contribution. But what's in a title?

1
BEING BEST

> Whatever you do, do from the heart, as for the
> Lord and not for others. Colossians 3:23

My father was born in 1948 and raised in Fond du Lac, Wisconsin, the same city I grew up in and where my mother still lives today. Its name in French means "foot of the lake" because of the city's position at the base or south end of Lake Winnebago—the largest lake in Wisconsin at almost 132,000 acres. Fond du Lac is a typical Midwestern city that feels smaller than its population of about forty-three thousand people.

My dad met my mom at a CYO (Catholic Youth Organization) dance when they were both barely teens. In the fall of 1967, my dad was drafted to serve his country in the Vietnam War. If not for failing a physical examination because of a previously

1

undetected condition, my dad would have joined anticommunist allies to support the South Vietnamese counter to the North Vietnamese, Soviet Union, and other communist allies. He made all the preparations to go. He said goodbye to his family and fiancée, got on a bus, and traveled about an hour south to Milwaukee. This is where he took, and failed, the physical. After getting sent back home, my dad had surgery to fix the ailment, married his sweetheart, and started a family. He was called to service again in the summer of 1968 and got a waiver because my mom was pregnant with my older sister.

I came along four years later in 1972. President Nixon called for the withdrawal of US troops from Vietnam in 1973, and the war officially ended with the fall of Saigon in 1975.

I heard the story about my dad almost going to Vietnam a handful of times as a child without ever stopping to recognize the magnitude of it. If my parents were captivated by how close my dad had been to going to war, they never showed it. As an adult with a wife and children, I think about it and can't get the precariousness out of my mind. And I fully know if my dad would have gone to Vietnam to serve his country, it would have set in motion a series of events undoubtedly changing the time of his marriage (assuming he made it home alive) and subsequent children. In other words, I would not exist if my dad had not failed that physical.

And it wasn't even a big, scary medical problem that caused it. I recall it being a hernia. My mom can't remember, and my dad has since passed away so he cannot resolve the debate. But in my mind, I am alive on this earth because my dad failed a physical exam due to a hernia. I suppose I could send away for a copy of the Selective Service System records to verify the facts, but I like remembering it this way.

I can't even imagine how different things would have been if my dad had gone to Vietnam. Life as I know it: vanished! For me, that failed physical was a gift from God—the gift of life. It is up to me to detect what He had in store for me with that priceless gift and this one wildly precious life.

My dad had a long career in the grocery business and had been, in many ways, defined by his career. He proudly worked for Schultz Sav-O Stores in Sheboygan, a city on the shores of Lake Michigan about forty-five minutes east of Fond du Lac.

Schultz Sav-O distributed food and other grocery items through franchised and corporate retail supermarkets, which operated under the name Piggly Wiggly. To people who knew him, my dad was synonymous with Piggly Wiggly. He loved what he did, never complained about work, and was loyal to his company. I often joked that he had a big pig tattoo on his chest. He worked for the company for over thirty-five years. Yet he always told me that people will remember you for who you are as a person and not what you do for a living. After all, what's in a title?

During my youth, I must have spent hundreds of hours standing at my father's side as he carried on conversations that seemed like would never end. Invariably, errands to the service station or local home improvement center would lead to my dad running into an acquaintance, co-worker, old neighbor, bowling buddy, or high school classmate he had not seen in years. And there I'd be, a relatively quiet child, resisting all temptation to plead with my father for us to leave. I waited at his heels amazed that there could be so much to talk about. My dad, as the joke would go, could be dropped by helicopter in the middle of Timbuktu and in short order run into someone he knew. His hobbies introduced him to an array of people from diverse walks of life. He connected with them all. His work kept him traveling rather frequently from grocery store to grocery store throughout Wisconsin and northern Illinois. Again, he met quite a few people and built a rapport with all of them.

My dad's mission at each grocery store, grossly overgeneralized and oversimplified, was to affect change. He learned the best way to do that was to start with the person. My dad believed employees are more influenced by relationship than by policy or procedure. He didn't have a college education and worked his way up through the ranks from humble beginnings as a butcher. But he had a way of making people feel comfortable with him.

I didn't appreciate it until I got much older, but the lesson I learned in my youth from my father was how important it is to put work into meaningful relationships. He was a CXO.

I have always put a lot of pressure on myself to do my best and do meaningful things with my life. When I was younger, I feared failure and had to remind myself to try new things even if it seemed I would not be successful. To some extent, I believe I tried not to disappoint my dad, my earthly father. I wanted to be a CXO apple from the CXO tree. As a teenager and young adult, I wasn't self-aware enough to articulate it in terms of me trying to be the best person I could be or as created in God's image. But looking back on it, I believe I had been hungering to be the person God created me to be. I didn't want to disappoint my heavenly Father. I was raised a Christian and had great examples of Christianity around me. But to be honest, as a child and teenager, my relationship with God was just something I felt obligated to do. I didn't have intentionality.

At age eighteen, I struggled to find myself and what I wanted to do with my life. I knew it was an expectation I go to college, but I didn't have a strong inclination on where I should go. I chose the University of Wisconsin in Oshkosh, about thirty minutes north of Fond du Lac. My older sister was a student there, so it seemed like as good a choice as any.

Let me immediately and unequivocally say I met my wife in college and, if for no other reason than that, I was meant to go there. She has been my best friend for over twenty-five years. But after about a year and a half of less than stellar grades and fragile friendships, I had been feeling down and out. I didn't like learning by the traditional classroom style, and I didn't understand how to study in college, which diverges from high school. I changed majors three times. And having roommates was difficult for me because I am introverted and a little set in my own ways.

I got an unexpected greeting card from my mom to lift my spirits. My mom is empathetic and good at reading people's emotions; maybe because of mother's intuition, she recognized I needed a boost in my spirits. I don't remember what the cover of the card said or looked like, and I don't know where the card is today. But I am 100% certain the card contained the following phrase inside: "Being best doesn't mean being better than anyone else, it means being the best you can be." I have never forgotten that message, and I regularly repeat it to myself as positive self-talk. In fact, it has become spiritual to me; I pray and meditate on it. My lifelong self-imposed pressure to DO my best was really me wanting to BE my best and as created in God's image. In fact, at about the time I got this greeting card from my mom I started regularly going to mass on campus because I chose to, and wanted to, not because anyone expected me. For me, being my best meant putting work into my relationship with God.

Also at about this same time in college, I started a part-time job at a sporting goods store. On the day I applied (and was immediately interviewed) for the position, I met Rick, the store manager. A big guy, both in stature and personality, Rick could be intimidating. I remember him asking me what type of putter my dad golfed with. I had deflected the conversation to my dad because I felt embarrassed by my modest clubs, whose brand was thrift shop and not pro shop. A golf fanatic and avid club collector, Rick took an interest in what make and model clubs you played with. It was a simple way for him to connect with people. In my case, he wanted to see me upgrade my set as soon as possible. He unselfishly took care of that by giving me a set of MacGregor DX Tourney irons from his collection. Though from the 1960's, they are a timeless classic and certainly an improvement from what I had been playing with. We spent hundreds of hours together on the golf course where I learned invaluable lessons about leadership, parenthood, and friendship.

Rick was a tough boss, yet always recognized your efforts. He had high expectations and would let you know when they weren't met. A pleaser by nature, I found it rather easy to comply with his standards and enjoyed the acknowledgment that would follow. He extended more trust and opportunity to me as I proved myself, and I felt very proud of the contributions I made.

Rick could swiftly make connections with customers and that contributed to success with sales. He helped me become more confident in my sales and presentation skills. I owe much of the confidence I have in my role as a public speaker to his grooming. I learned to be proficient at giving sales pitches; my favorite were for golf clubs and inline skates, which were all the rage in the early-1990's. Each purchase took a fair amount of customer education and I was happy to oblige. I can remember customers telling me they weren't ready to buy, but they really enjoyed hearing me talk about the product. That was the first time I can recall feeling like I could connect with people.

Rick was a competitive person and when all the work had been completed, we would have friendly contests such as putting golf balls to a target on the floor, tossing Nerf footballs to a target on the wall, or playing bumper pool (until, to our disappointment, the table sold). For all of his efforts, he got a twenty-year-old college student to work every Friday, Saturday, and Sunday for three years. I enjoyed every moment of it. Little did I recognize it, he had put considerable effort into building a constructive relationship with me. He was a CXO.

Despite the positive examples, when I was a much younger adult, I did not value relationships like I do today. My dad's lessons hadn't sunk in yet. I did not put enough work into relationships. Against my dad's advice, I had been more concerned about what I did for a living than who I had been as a person. I remember telling a co-worker at my first "real job" out of college I didn't have a job to make friends. I took pride in being principled, direct, and right. I am not sure why I used to be that way other than that I was a young and immature male and my stubborn German ancestry. One example is when (before getting the greeting card from my mom) my college Educational Psychology professor called on me during class and while doing so used the name "Danny." I had been whispering with a classmate sitting next to me and not fully paying attention. I took the name Danny as an implication I had been acting like a child and being scolded. Only my grandmother, aunts, and uncles still called me Danny, and they did so because it was habit for them—as a child I was called Danny. I responded to the professor during class in front of everyone saying, "Why did you call me Danny?" She replied with, "Isn't that your name?" To which I said, "No. My name is Dan!" And I said it with all the tone I could muster to imply "DUH!" Needless to say I had been invited to stay after class where the professor cried profusely and chastised me for embarrassing her (her department chairperson was in the room observing and evaluating her). She said Danny was a "term of endearment." True or not, I severely lacked awareness and appreciation of the fact it mattered how I treated people. I certainly wouldn't respond that way today. But at the time it was more important I not be called a name I associated with being a misbehaving child in front of my peers.

Customer service is another area where I often lacked proper judgment and took the cliché "The customer is always right" to an extreme. This behavior manifested from high expectations for how people should do their jobs (my dad always taught me to take pride in my work) and modeling from my mom. As a youth I admired the way she handled herself on the phone with nuisance telemarketers. My mom taught me the virtue of justice, and to stand up for what I believe in. When I felt I had been right and treated unjustly by a customer service representative (e.g.

cashier), I often shared my point of view in strongly worded rants void of emotional intelligence. I gave no leeway for ineptitude, unexpected circumstances, or honest mistakes.

As newlyweds, my wife and I almost went without hot water because, on principle, I didn't want to pay for the purchase and installation of a water heater that was higher than the quote I received. I am embarrassed to say an unbending, guileless phone call to the owner of the plumbing company solved the matter. Yes, there are more than a few service providers out there who I owe an apology to. I was a faux CXO who wasn't trying as hard as I could to be the best I could be. I am glad to say I am a recovering angry, entitled customer.

God calls me to be the best person I can be—not better than anyone else. That is why I am so fascinated by being a CXO—the best example of myself. Being a CXO is really about being the best YOU imaginable. It means you have the power to choose how you conduct yourself and how you treat people. The most profound change in my life came when I made the realization that the meaning of life is not about power, pleasure, or control.

The meaning of life is to live with a purpose; by putting work into relationships and loving others. The true meaning of life is connecting with people.

I have been exhibiting CXO-like behavior for several years, albeit inconsistently and without ever naming it. Categorizing the attributes and putting a construct to them has increased my ambition to be a CXO regularly and reliably. In this book I aim to provide a simple model for how you can live with purpose and meaning, which will help to satisfy part of your inherent emotional needs and spiritual hungers. I spell it out in the context of a job description because it is something everyone can make relevant to them. The dignity of work is innate to who we are as humans. We are called to respect each profession and its value to our communities just as we are called to respect each person. We define our existence—get a sense of self-image—by what we do. Our work becomes our identity. Pope Francis once wrote that "Work is a necessity, part of the meaning of life on earth, a path to growth, human development and fulfillment." Paid employees, parents, or even volunteers who are not getting paid for their work can all actualize the benefits of growth, development, and fulfillment.

We all perform better when we know what is expected of us because it gives us motivation and something to measure ourselves against. A job description clearly spells out the requirements and expectations of a role, without ambiguity or misinterpretation. So, on the pages that follow, I share the job description of a CXO—Chief Experience Officer. I hope it helps to encourage you and lead you closer to filling your desire to live a life of purpose and meaning and be the best you can be. I am confident it will help you connect with people. It has changed my life and I believe it can change yours. The book is the apex of my journey from the child of a grocer, meandering teen, to unaware young adult, maturing man, and eventually a self-actualizing Christian. I learned about myself, chose to live with more purpose, and love courageously. I want the same for you.

I hope you embrace your journey and learn how to more effectively unleash the potential inside you. I have included reflection questions at the end of each chapter to further open the orifices of your heart and augment your learning.

Chapter 1 Reflection Questions

1. To what extent do you believe you were uniquely created, and in God's image?
2. Are you most motivated by power, pleasure, or purpose? And what influenced you to have that motivation?

JOB DESCRIPTION

POSITION TITLE: CXO – Chief Experience Officer
REPORTS TO: Values
SUPERVISES: Choices
CLASSIFICATION: Full Time/ Unpaid/ Complete Benefits

POSITION SUMMARY

The Chief Experience Officer delivers exemplary, life-changing experiences to family, friends, co-workers and any other person he or she interacts with on a day-to-day basis. The CXO is a driving factor in determining the merit of someone else's human experience. Without bias or fuss, the CXO will influence the morale, loyalty, engagement, satisfaction, and self-worth of others.

PRINCIPAL DUTIES

1. Listen more than you talk.
2. Say nice things in a nice way.
3. Show appreciation to others.
4. Be patient with others.
5. Forgive others.
6. Apologize when you make a mistake.
7. Follow through on what you say you are going to do.
8. Sacrifice your time, money, or effort for the sake of someone else.
9. Leave all things better than you found them.
10. Seek the common good over your individual good.

REQUIREMENTS

No experience necessary.

CORE COMPETENCIES

- Approachability
- Positivity
- Authenticity
- Vulnerability
- Humility
- Generosity

PHYSICAL/SENSORY DEMANDS

Must be able to withstand extended periods of peace and joy. Occasional light lifting of arms to give hugs and pats on the back. Exposure to slight cheek pain due to prolonged smiling.

To view online or print go to www.danimatedonline.com/resources

2

THE CAPTION

Make no mistake: God is not mocked,

for a person will reap only what he sows.

Galatians 6:7

POSITION TITLE: CXO—Chief Experience Officer

In this context, by "experience" I mean contact with, exposure to, and to encounter. It refers to the experiences that others have with you; how you connect with others. Putting it another way, in this role you will be the Chief Officer of others' exposure and encounters—experience—with you. Remember, short title and big contribution. You reap what you sow.

REPORTS TO: Values

Your values are your boss. A CXO's values are his or her guiding principles. For your values to be your guide it presumes you have done values clarification. If you are not clear on what the top three or five personal values are that guide your decisions and actions I would recommend you do that right away. There is a simple three-step process for values clarification I developed called DETERMINE-DEFINE-DRIVE in the appendix of this book.

When making decisions or faced with challenges as a CXO, your values will be something secure and comfortable to rely on. You may not be clear on what you should do or what the best answer is, but you can certainly stay aligned to your values. And you will sleep better at night for doing so. I used to beat myself up with remorse afterward for how I treated people; at the moment I didn't see it. Earlier, when I shared that I used to make a hobby out of letting service providers know "the customer is always right," I was not acting in tandem with my values. Had I considered it, I would have made a different choice—and had much less regret. It takes discipline and self-awareness, but your values are your values for a reason; you hold them deeply. When we don't act in alignment with our values, it creates dissonance and pushes away joy.

A number of years ago a driver behind me honked her horn because she thought I had stopped too long at a red light waiting to make a right-hand turn. In my mind I was clearly in the right. My first reaction may have been to honk back, make an obscene gesture, or say something critical about her to my daughter who was in the car with me. Instead, I paused and contemplated my values. I report to them. I did not do those destructive behaviors and assumed the best of the woman who honked at me. I was glad I did when we both pulled into the same parking lot to drop our kids off at day-care. It would have been easy for either of us to react when her daughter shouted to me, "My mommy was honking at you!" It was a little awkward, but I had no regrets about how I conducted myself and the other woman didn't escalate the matter further. A couple weeks later we both ended up at the same holiday party; she is a friend of one of my family members. How fortunate that we both acted with integrity and respect. We could laugh it off and move forward.

Consonance between your values and day-to-day actions is not always easy. Your values are your boss, and just like dealing with your literal boss it can be difficult. Reporting to your values takes courage. I remember one time when I had been coaching my son's baseball team and in one particular game we had a big lead. This was a recreation league and meant to be more developmental than competitive. I was an aspiring CXO, and I had told the team there is no need to unnecessarily run up the score; that we wanted to be respectful to the other team. Respect is one of my personal values. At some point the players, who were around eleven years old, stopped paying attention to the first and third-base coaches and tried to score at all costs. We yelled at them to stop and they would run right by. Players were trying to stretch an easy double into an unnecessary home run, all while we were ahead by a considerable amount. Between innings I gave the players a stern talking to about how disappointed I was, told them they weren't conducting themselves as men, and that the team across the field deserved to be treated with respect. We either needed to change our actions now or forfeit the game. And before the next pitch was thrown, I walked across the diamond and apologized to the coach of the other team. It would have been easier to let things continue as is, but I knew it wasn't the right thing to do. I think some of the parents of my players presumed I was crazy, but I report to my values.

SUPERVISES: Choices

A CXO oversees his or her choices. You have the power to choose and are accountable for your choices. When someone says something rude to you, when you get cut-off in traffic, or when you get accolades for a job well-done, you make the choice of how you will respond. Will you respond with harsh words in vengeance or will you exercise restraint and grace? Will you respond with angry road-rage or show poise and self-control? Will you show humility and gratitude or conceit and self-righteousness? Isn't that awesome? You get to choose!

The fact that I oversee my choices was difficult to accept when my father passed away unexpectedly, in 2008, at the young age of sixty. I wanted to be angry and sad because of the circumstance; even better if the world stopped and waited for me to heal. Alas, life went on. I had unfinished business with my dad and it frustrated me I couldn't get closure. Add to that, I loved the person I was becoming as I got older and wiser, and I wish my dad had gotten a chance to see the man I had grown to be. Don't get me wrong, my father and I loved each other, and we knew it; yet I would do things differently if I had the chance. And I would tell him things if I could, like how I now understand the highs and lows of being a father, husband, employee, Christian, home owner, and community member. It is difficult work—especially if you want to be any good at it. Today, I am more equipped to appreciate what he went through. Finally, I needed to realize I had been choosing to be angry and sad. I had the power to respond differently. This is a challenging truth to accept and when you can it is life changing. I still experience brief periods of sadness and mourning, but it no longer owns me.

Everyone faces a different set of life circumstances; that is where we differ. What we all have in common is that we get to choose how we react to those circumstances. A CXO will not deflect accountability or responsibility. We cannot control what types of situations and circumstances arise in our lives, but we all can control how we react to them. A CXO responds to situations as aligned to his or her values.

CLASSIFICATION: Full Time/ Unpaid/ Complete Benefits

You can and should aspire to work full-time as a CXO, but it is not required. If you take an hour, a day, or even a year off you can restart without hesitation.

As CXO, you do not get paid in the customary form of the word. The role is unpaid in the literal sense. But you get the full benefit of a life of purpose and meaning. Our purpose is to connect with others—to serve others. "Just so, the Son of Man did not come to be served but to serve and to give his life as a ransom for many." (Matthew 20:28) By turning the focus away from you and towards others, the rewards are rich and bountiful.

Chapter 2 Reflection Questions

1. Who are the family, friends, co-workers, and other individuals you interact with most on a daily basis?
2. What personal values guide your thoughts, words, and actions?
3. Are you more likely to take ownership for your actions or assume the victim role and cast blame? And why?

3
DO GOOD

We must consider how to rouse one another to love and good works. Hebrews 10:24

Let me be transparent and straightforward in saying I am not a CXO; at least not full-time. I have my moments and consider myself in a part-time or temporary position. If I were to receive a performance appraisal for my work as a CXO it would read "Needs Improvement." I am on this journey with you and do not come from a place of condescension or self-righteousness. What I can tell you—and I want to be abundantly clear on this—is when I am being effective in the role of CXO it has transformative effects on my life and those around me. I have seen the view from both ends of the executive wing and it is definitely better in the CXO office.

I know I feel good when I do good things for others. I believe we all are called to do all the good we can. The gifts we are blessed with are meant to be shared. "Nor do they light a lamp and then put it under a bushel basket; it is set on a lamp-stand, where it gives light to all in the house." (Matthew 5:15) Wanting to do good things, and be a good person, makes us virtuous people. Many Christians do good things because we want a seat at God's table in heaven. Being an example of Christian morality serves the global purpose of making this world a little better place and informs the day-to-day actions of a CXO. Let's take a look at a summary of the position.

POSITION SUMMARY

The Chief Experience Officer delivers exemplary, life-changing experiences to family, friends, co-workers, and any other person he or she interacts with on a day-to-day basis. The CXO is a driving factor in determining the merit of someone else's human experience. Without bias or fuss, the CXO will influence the morale, loyalty, engagement, satisfaction, and self-worth of others.

This summary is worthy of added explanation. To start,

let's look at the word "exemplary." To be exemplary means you are a model of what is ideal and desirable. You could say it is commendable and worthy of imitation, just as we are called to imitate the example of Christ. Next, I want to draw your attention to the second paragraph, "The CXO is a driving factor in determining the merit of someone else's human experience." Reflect on that for a moment. I am talking about changing lives. The potential is rather extraordinary when you think about it. You have the power to make someone's day. I remember the first time another adult told me in an email I had made his day because of something kind I had written to him. I took that very factually (regardless of whether that was his intention or not) and often remind myself such a level of influence exists within me. Contemplate it, you can quite literally make someone's day.

Lastly, I want to touch on the phrase "without bias or fuss." Charles Dickens once said, "Do all the good you can, and make as little fuss about it as possible." I love that quote, it speaks to the brilliance of being a CXO. Try to give a positive experience to everyone regardless of age, nationality, race, or any other discriminating factor; and part of being a CXO means you do so without fanfare or shouting it from atop a mountain. Jesus is a perfect example of that; it is often expressed in scripture how he would retreat to a quiet place to pray after performing a miracle. CXOs don't do it for the glory or attention. They do it because they believe they are called to be virtuous.

Effective CXOs will influence the self-worth and satisfaction of others. I have been transformed in every instance where I encountered a CXO; it is life-giving and healing. I have the power to do the same onto others—as do you. Take advantage of every chance possible to be the face of Christ to someone else. God gives us the platform and we need to be alert and attentive to notice it.

Chapter 3 Reflection Questions

1. What gets in the way of you regularly trying to let your light shine and sharing your gifts with others?
2. When you help others, is it important you get external recognition or are you intrinsically motivated?

4
I CAN DO THIS

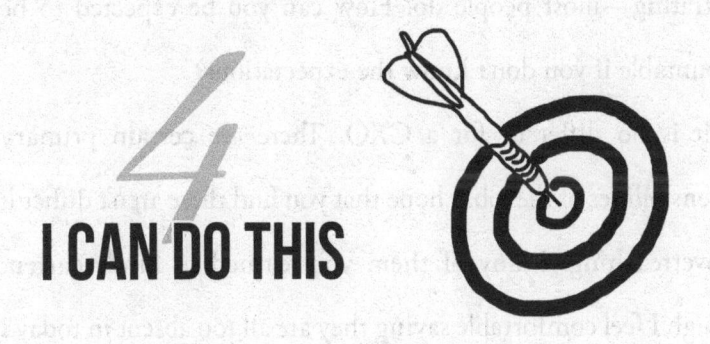

I have the strength for everything through him
who empowers me. Philippians 4:13

In order to do anything well, you must be clear on what is expected of the role. When you are fuzzy on the details of what success looks like, you will not have the direction needed to achieve it nor will you have the metrics to evaluate how you are doing in the role.

It is helpful to know what is expected of members of a family, church, community, or any other communal experience. In your family you might set the expectation for respectful communication. Members of a church are aware there is an expectation for stewardship. In the workplace, well I am sure you can relate to an experience where your employer or boss didn't clarify expectations of you. I assume you felt that was frustrating—most people do. How can you be expected to be accountable if you don't know the expectations?

It is no different for a CXO. There are certain primary responsibilities of the job. I hope that you find these aren't difficult or overreaching. Many of them you learned in kindergarten. Though I feel comfortable saying they are all too absent in today's world. Admittedly, there are other behaviors that are CXO-like and appreciated by others. These ten practices promise to get you there effectively and efficiently.

PRINCIPAL DUTIES

1. Listen more than you talk

Listening is something we have been doing since birth and for many of us we have been listening improperly for just as long. Faux CXOs will use listening simply as a pause to wait for their turn to talk. When, instead, a more effective approach is to take the time and truly try to understand the other person. Genuine listening is the essence of understanding. Don't respond with your own stories of your own experiences. Just listen.

Think about the last time a friend told you about a vacation they went on. Did you tell them about your own vacation experience? Or what about the last time an acquaintance shared with you a struggle they were having at work. Did you tell them what you did in a similar circumstance? Often others will merely want you to listen. Or maybe you know a person who has seen everything you have seen and done everything you have done? As you share your experiences, they are interjecting with their own stories about how they have "been there, done that." It is a psychological game of one-upmanship and likely frustrating to you.

I am a fixer by nature; I seek closure and try to solve others' problems. I need to be mindful and remember not to move too quickly. I made that mistake with friends in the past and they felt judged and invalidated.

Listening requires us to understand not only the words others are sharing but also the feelings behind those words. Listening attentively means you are watching body language and picking up on tone of voice. Someone can say one thing and mean another; pay attention to the cues.

When you talk, ask powerful questions. Great questions have

an almost mystical power to unlock meaning, perspective, and empathy. The question shows the other person you want to invest the time in understanding them better rather than expecting them to understand you. Show someone you value them by asking a question that gets them to look deeper into the recesses of their experience. If you are unsure what type of questions to ask, try these simple ideas: "Tell me more," and "What else?" Both are short responses with a big contribution.

2. Say nice things in a nice way

You have heard the cliché hundreds, if not thousands, of times before. "It is not what you say it's how you say it." True, and I think what you say matters as well. Words carry great power. No single thing can ruin the credibility of a CXO faster than using an ill-placed word. Effective CXOs are self-aware and use positive language in positive ways. Words can cause tears and break hearts. Said in the right way, words can light fires and build bridges. I am sure you have heard this cliché before too, "If you have nothing nice to say don't say it at all." This is a good rule of thumb for CXOs.

I remember one occasion I had hired a new employee, and I

was touring her around one facility we operated. I introduced her to a Director in the organization and, in greeting him, she told him how much she loved his smile. It's true; he has a great smile, I never thought to tell him that. When he heard this compliment, his whole face lit up and you could tell she made his day. She was genuine and sincere and immediately established a connection with him.

3. Show appreciation to others

As humans, we often second guess ourselves, question our value, compare ourselves to others, and feel self-conscious. CXOs put others at ease by showing them they appreciate them for who they are.

I am a huge believer in the healing power of gratitude. Occasional five-minute gratitude vacations during the day, where you reflect on all the people and things you are grateful for, will help a CXO cope when life seems to close in on them. Or journaling; try keeping a gratitude journal to reflect on all of the gifts God has blessed you with.

Beyond your own private gratitude practices, be sure to openly let others know you appreciate them. Be specific and use the other person's name. Such as, "Bill, I appreciate your attention to detail." Not only will you make someone's day by telling them how you appreciate them, but studies have proven that it will make you happier as well when you share it.

In the spring of 2011, at a charity auction, I was the winning bidder on a dinner party from a well-known local restaurant for thirty people valued at thirty dollars per head. If you are doing the math, that is a nine-hundred dollar value. I was very excited—I paid well below the face-value for the dinner package and I had a party with thirty of my closest friends in my near future.

After winning, my wife and I had numerous conversations about how to best use the dinner. A big bash with our friends would surely be fun. We thought about inviting family for a reunion of sorts. We thought about having the dinner party coincide with some holiday and killing the proverbial "two birds with one stone." A birthday celebration for our kids was another idea (their special days are only three weeks apart). And then it hit us. We should use this opportunity to honor all the people in our life who we were thankful for. So, on a beautiful July evening we hosted a "Gratitude Dinner."

Our guest list consisted of the thirty family members, friends, co-workers, mentors, and servant leaders who profoundly impacted our lives more so than any others. It was a difficult decision; we had a finite number of seats and made the tough choice to leave people off the invite list that would have seemed like an obvious choice to an outsider. At the dinner we gave them each a hand written note detailing what they had done for us and how they had made a positive difference in our lives. The reaction from our guests to the evening was magical and overwhelming. To this day, my wife and I name that night as one of the best nights of our twenty-plus years together.

To be clear, my point is not to grand stand about how nice it was for us to do this, or even to highlight how special our guests felt (though that had been a great result). The point I want to emphasize is how meaningful the process was of contemplating all of the people we had crossed paths with and to examine the influence they had on us. That was the most spectacular part—the exercise of thinking about all of the people who we were grateful for, why, and counting our blessings for how they had made a difference in our lives. We had never done anything like that before; writing down specific things people had done that we were grateful for and sharing it with them. Frankly, it was emotional and we shed a tear or two in the process.

4. Forgive others

God calls us to "Be merciful, just as [also] your Father is merciful." (Luke 6:36) It is a reminder that CXOs will be forgiven by God for their transgressions and CXOs should forgive others likewise. Carrying grudges will prohibit you from being able to be a genuine CXO. Lack of forgiveness will show in your demeanor; it impedes vulnerability. If you want to see a relationship that is troubled undergo authentic transformation, try forgiveness.

In December of 2015, Pope Francis initiated an extraordinary Holy Year, or Jubilee, for the Catholic Church in the succeeding twelve months. The "Year of Mercy," as it is known, encouraged believers to embrace the mercy of God and seek forgiveness of their sins. Whether Catholic or not, all Christians can appreciate the benefits of practicing mercy. Each New Year, rather than establishing a resolution, I pick a word to focus on in my prayers and quiet reflections. I chose "mercy" in 2016 to leverage the

Pope's intention. Each day as I concentrated on mercy I realized how much bitterness I carried. I forgave people selectively and discriminatorily. Eventually I could feel my heart soften. The lack of compassion I showed for certain people different from me prohibited me from delivering exemplary, life-changing experiences. The more merciful I became the better CXO I became.

We live in a world of so much civil discord, hate, and intolerance. Mercy is the great elixir. Carrying resentment and contempt in your heart impedes the true work of a CXO. Your capacity to forgive is in direct proportion to your longevity as a CXO.

When you find yourself unbending to forgive the missteps of others, try remembering this simple shift in paradigms—believe others are trying their best. Remember that, in most cases, people are not trying to fail. Believing in someone else will usually result in that person believing in you. The more people believe in one another the easier it is to forgive one another.

5. Apologize when you make a mistake

If a CXO forgives others, they would want others to forgive them. Start with an apology. The CXO position doesn't come with the requirement that they will always make the right decisions. An apology creates mutual understanding and empathy.

Some faux CXOs believe admitting a mistake is a sign of weakness; their egos get in the way. Nothing could be further from the truth. Real CXOs create credibility and empathy by acknowledging their shortcomings. And if you want to try something really life-changing, apologize to someone who by social standards has a position below you such as an employee who reports to you, or your children. I work at catching myself when I tell my kids to do as I say, not as I do. I own up to my shortcomings as a parent; I am not an expert at it and I can take an honest look in the mirror.

An apology tells the other person that you are on the same plane as them; that you are on the same journey as they are. "I am sorry" means I want to be better; I want to be the best I can be.

6. Be patient with others

We live in a world where information is coming at us so fast by the time we process it the variables change. Many faux CXOs suffer from hurry sickness. Increasing demands and the spawn of technology have created a climate where patience equals inactivity and underachievement.

CXOs are tolerant and believe others are trying their best. Show others you value them by giving them the time to process, learn, and apply. People are resilient and CXOs find that people usually rise to the level of expectation when given the appropriate time to do so.

It is easy to be patient when everything and everyone is going our way. A factor that causes impatience is our unwillingness to accept people different from us. If your family, teammates, and friends are the same as you then things would probably move faster. Faster is not always better. Embrace diversity, be patient, and reap the rewards of superior results.

One way I increase my patience with others is through prayer. When I catch myself getting impatient with others, I replace that behavior with prayer. I pray that I show more tolerance and acceptance, and I pray a prayer of gratitude for the other person.

At the start of my day I pray when I know I will encounter someone who I have had difficulty being patient with in the past. If I have a meeting with a challenging co-worker, I pray about it before the meeting and more often than not the interaction goes much smoother than in the past.

7. Follow through on what you say you are going to do

The essence of integrity is follow-through. CXOs can be counted on and are dependable. "I will call you later. I'll get that to you tomorrow. I will be at your place by eight o'clock. You can tell me anything. I won't tell anyone else." These are all simply words without the requisite follow-through.

Have you experienced the situation where you call, email, or message someone to check on the status of an unresolved situation and the other person replies with, "I was just about to contact you?" Isn't it fascinating how faux CXOs are always "just about" to follow up with you? A true CXO will follow up without being reminded.

A repeated pattern of not doing what you say will make you a faux CXO. Eventually people will stop looking to you. It is difficult to be an effective CXO when others are actively trying to avoid you.

A CXO feels emotionally committed and has psychological ownership for anything he or she promised no matter how important or trivial. If a CXO cannot deliver, he or she will look for alternate ways to achieve the same end, or ways to make it up to the person who was let down. After repeated evidence of dependability others will come to you based on your stellar reputation.

8. Sacrifice your time, money, or effort for the sake of someone else

It has been my experience that the more I focus on my own needs and interests the more discontent and irritable I become. The more I focus on others the more at peace I am. A CXO recognizes that sometimes we need to distract ourselves from ourselves. At the times when I feel at my lowest or when life gets just a little too overwhelming for me, I sacrifice for others. I always feel better when I do. It can be as simple as offering to help someone with a task they are working on, complimenting someone, or buying someone an unexpected cup of coffee.

And by definition, a sacrifice means it might not be easy. It might even hurt just a little. CXOs don't give in a shallow way, they give profoundly. Faux CXOs will sacrifice for their own gain; they want to look good externally or expect something in return for their faux generosity. They give only out of their excess.

Be the driving factor that determines the merit of someone else's human experience by giving your time, talent, and treasures to others. Look to any church or local non-profit organization and you will find a plethora of examples of people serving others. Volunteering is fundamental to a fulfilling life because you recognize the beauty that comes from being a part of something bigger than you. God calls us to help those less fortunate than we are. "Amen, I say to you, what you did not do for one of these least ones, you did not do for me." (Matthew 25:45)

9. Leave all things better than you found them

CXOs want others to feel like they are better off for knowing them. Make all things, and I mean all things, better because of your involvement; relationships, projects, and the environment. This will take work and CXOs aren't afraid of getting their hands dirty. All people and places are God's creation and we should care for them.

Faux CXOs focus only on problems and negativity. They feel like they are adding value by only pointing out what is wrong. I have seen dozens of new leaders come into organizations and try to push their agenda without ever connecting with the people. They try to make their mark by accomplishing a high profile initiative or project without understanding the nuances of the culture. As initiatives failed and those leaders eventually were replaced, the cost of starting and restarting took its toll on morale and the bottom line. I have seen people enter new friendships only focused on their own troubles, needs, or accomplishments; never allowing for reciprocity. Faux CXOs will try to have their hands in everything and share opinions without being constructive or adding value. Faux CXOs seem to thrive on making a mess of things and then walking out and leaving others to deal with the wreckage. Real CXOs are solution focused. A CXO appreciates that their legacy will be built on the capacity to transform people, places, and things virtuously.

As a kid I spend many hours in the garage with my dad helping him clean, polish, and perform minor repairs on his 1969 Chevrolet Corvette. I learned certain etiquette around classic cars. Because of my proven sensibility, I got to drive the car as young as fifteen years old. And when I was seventeen, my dad's friend let me drive his 1971 Corvette convertible. When some of his peer group thought he was crazy and asked why he would let me do that, he said he had no problem with it because, "Dan would probably bring it back washed, waxed, and in better condition than when he left with it." My parents taught me the lesson at a young age to leave things better than you found them—it has served me well.

10. Seek the common good over your individual good

Faux CXOs are selfish and believe the more others have the less there is for them. A true CXO is unselfish and believes there is enough to go around for everyone.

In the workplace they are called "silos." In silos, departments do not work collaboratively with others. Rather, they consider what is most convenient for them. In the sports world it is called a "ball hog." In friend groups they are called "cliques." We live in a world where too many people practice relativism, individualism, and hedonism. If it feels good and helps us at the moment, then we do it.

Earlier in my career I worked as part of a small two-person team; just me and my boss. She left the organization to pursue other opportunities and most people, including me, thought I would automatically be promoted into the vacated management position. I was shocked and hurt when I was not. Someone from outside the organization had been hired, and I had a choice to make; I could work with her and help her be successful or I could let my disappointment cause me to sabotage her efforts in an attempt to make me look like the better option. I had a friend who just lost his job. With that perspective, I decided it is better to be grateful for what I have than to lament over what I don't have. My new boss had a choice as well; she could do everything in her power to make me look bad or she could leverage me to help her achieve the desired results. We both choose to be CXOs and our team excelled to new heights because of it. She put effort into developing me and advocated for me to get promoted into a newly created position. Eventually, she left the organization, and

I was selected to take over the management position. Had I acted in resentment years earlier I may never have gotten the chance.

I cannot think of a single example of a time in my life when acting on the good of one yielded a long-term positive effect. Granted, the example probably exists; someone who is seen as courageous and visionary. But my experience has been that the common good leads to more peace and joy in my life than focusing on what is good for solely me. Personal wins fade quickly but team wins endure.

Chapter 4 Reflection Questions

1. Do you often dominate conversations?
2. Do you have regular practices of gratitude?
3. In what ways do you share your gifts (time, talent, and treasure) with others?

5
WAIT, CAN I DO THIS?

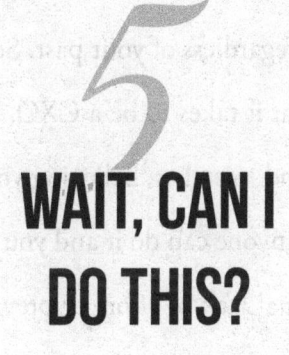

> Trust in the Lord with all your heart, on your own intelligence do not rely. Proverbs 3:5

We are called to be holy. And in our own brokenness we are holy. The role of a CXO isn't reserved for those who hold some unrealistic candle for excellence and flawlessness. It is in our brokenness we recognize our need for a Savior. It is in our brokenness we exemplify the fortitude and providence that Jesus taught us. Most of the best CXOs out there have compelling stories of hardships, missteps, and restarts. The point is, anyone can be a CXO and you can start anytime.

REQUIREMENTS: No experience necessary

The requirements of the position of CXO are none. The grace of God allows you to start anytime regardless of your past. Some people may wonder if they have what it takes to be a CXO. You may think about all of your faults and mistakes, believing you're not a qualified person. I assure you anyone can do it and you can start anytime. Any perceived or actual lack of effort or previous success will not prevent you from being a CXO; if you slip along the way that is okay. You can restart in your role at any time. It's never too late to make a difference in the lives of others.

When I was six years old and first wanted to get a book from the library, I needed to get a library card. In middle school, when I wanted to take part in athletics, I needed to go to my doctor and have a physical examination. Driving a car, of course, meant getting a license. Attaining a job after college meant a criminal background check was mandatory. When I got married, a marriage license was required. Buying a home necessitated financing approval and a subsequent home inspection. When I was ready to be a dad it required nothing; becoming a parent is easy, requiring no accreditations or prerequisites. Being a parent is hard, and you enter it with little or no experience. I am sure many first-time parents can relate to the feeling my wife and I had when we brought our first child home from the hospital. We looked at each other and asked, "Now what do we do?" The point is, just because we didn't have experience didn't mean we couldn't do it—and well. We knew it would not be easy, and we knew we were excited about the journey ahead.

When my oldest child was one-year-old my wife and I made the decision that one of us should stay home and focus on caring for our son rather than on a career. We had bad experiences with childcare and felt like we couldn't continue as full-time career minded individuals with a baby in the house. My wife is a teacher; she already had summers off and we carried her benefits package. So it made more sense for me to be the one to be a stay-at-home parent. I had no experience at this and wasn't sure if I had what it takes.

During my time as a stay-at-home dad, I took part-time jobs working evenings because we couldn't afford to live on only one salary—even without some of the luxuries like cable TV, taking vacations, and going out to dinner. I would leave the house for work around five-o'clock just as my wife was coming home. When I got home from work, she would be sound asleep. We eventually had a second child and for seven years we gave up much of our relationship together to do what we thought best for our children. As a stay-at-home dad I faced alienation from other moms. I remember one mom from my daughter's pre-school class wanted to set up a play-date with her daughter until she realized it would be me attending—not mom. I felt judged for my non-traditional decision. It shaped my understanding of compassion, being present, and service. It hurt at times; especially the lack of time my wife and I had together. I didn't always make the best parenting decisions nor have prior knowledge to rely on. But it was the best decision I ever made. Any demands, doubt, difficulties, and discouragement were washed away by an overwhelming sense of peace. It is one of the few times in my life when I knew for absolute certain I had done the right thing. No prior experience required. I would not be the father or husband I am today without that opportunity.

For years I had thought about learning to play the guitar. In truth, I wanted to KNOW HOW to play the guitar rather than LEARN HOW to play the guitar. I only had the endgame in mind. Finally, at forty-four years old and with no prior experience, I bought a used acoustic guitar and taught myself to play with the help of some online videos and tutorials. I realized it is never too late to start. I still wouldn't say I know how to play the guitar, but I am enjoying the process of learning to play the guitar. And sometimes I take a few days or a week off from practicing and I can get right back at it and still be learning to play. I am not an accomplished guitar player any more than I am an accomplished CXO. What I am doing is leaning into the voyage, as should you.

Chapter 5 Reflection Questions

1. What is an example of a time when you succeeded at something you had no previous experience doing? And how did that experience change you?
2. What are examples of ways you are holy in your brokenness?

6
THE HEART OF THE MATTER

Each must do as already determined, without sadness or compulsion, for God loves a cheerful giver. 2 Corinthians 9:7

There is what I call six little "itys" that will change your life and when implemented as a CXO will change the life of someone else. They are behaviors, attitudes, and skills—collectively called competencies—at the core of what it means to be a CXO. This list may sound familiar in ways to the principal duties, and they are. They are not mutually exclusive. The principal duties are the day-to-day tasks and activities required of the role. Mobilizing the competencies will aid you in carrying out the principal duties of a CXO successfully. For example, humility (competency) will help you sacrifice for the sake of others (principal duty) because it contributes to your selflessness. Keep in mind; you need not to do all six simultaneously to be a CXO. Doing any of them can influence the life of someone else. Also important to note is that the six are not an end point, meaning we are always working at them and trying to improve. Learning is a continuous journey.

CORE COMPETENCIES

Approachability

To be approachable means to be accessible and easy to talk to; people just like to have you around. Faux CXOs are insensitive to the interpersonal anxieties of others. I regularly work on that because I am quiet and reserved by nature. People who do not know me well may think I am standoffish. Maybe through a warm smile or a gracious welcome, I can invite others in and provide haven. I try to sense the emotions of those around me, anticipate their needs, and hear their unvoiced concerns. I also try to be mindful so that my non-verbal communication is sending the same message as my verbal communication.

One of the more approachable people I ever worked with had a simple technique she used. Whenever someone came to her office she would say, "Come in and sit down." It is genius in its simplicity. You never had to wonder if you were an interruption, unwanted, or valued. Immediately, by being invited to sit down, you would sense all anxiousness dissipate.

My paternal grandparents did not show approachability. When I was a child, they lived only one-block away from my house yet going over to visit always felt like an unwelcomed intrusion. Their front door would be locked, and after knocking they would come to the door and ask what you wanted—why were you there? The environment was sterile, awkward, and anxious. On the other hand, my maternal grandparents had an open door policy—literally. There always seemed to be someone visiting, and the environment felt tolerant, loving, and comfortable. My maternal grandparents were models of approachable CXOs. Some of my fondest childhood memories are from spending time with them. They gave me a sense of belongingness and acceptance. And though they lived a few miles away I spent much more time with them as a child than I did at my much closer, geographically, paternal grandparents. It is interesting to ponder how my dad flourished as a CXO from the examples he had.

Positivity

Positivity is the quality of being hopeful, optimistic, and faith-filled. CXOs see the good in others and speak in terms of possibilities and opportunities rather than take a victim mentality. Everyone knows a "negative Nancy" and has experienced when the life has been drawn out of a person or project because of the perpetual negativity. I have had people say, "You are so positive," in a tone to make it sound like it is a bad thing. Some people revel in negativity; complaining about people and situations rather than make things better. CXOs don't let others drag them down.

Positivity can be such a game changer because pessimism is the default instinct for many people. Negativity is assumed. Positive individuals can change those destructive patterns over time. People will be drawn to you because of your confidence and optimism, which will grow your influence as a CXO. Remember, you get to choose positivity if you want to regardless of the circumstances because as a CXO your choices report to you.

One simple technique that has worked for me is to limit my

use of the word "but" and insert "and" instead. The former can deflect accountability or make your audience defensive. The latter is inclusive and proactive. For example, suppose your boss says something like, "I agree that it is a short timeline BUT we will stick with the scheduled due date." It can give the perception the boss is dismissing your concerns. Now suppose your boss says, "I agree that it is a short timeline AND we will stick with the scheduled due date." The message is softened and generates less resistance from the listener. Plus, the speaker will feel inclined to add more detail (welcomed by the listener), such as why you need to stick with the scheduled due date. It may sound too simple; try it and I think you will be happy with the result.

Authenticity

Authenticity is pure, exposed, and genuine. People will know if you are authentic or not. If you have to tell someone you are authentic—you aren't. Perhaps this should be the first thing I mentioned in this book because without authenticity every other part of being a CXO is lost on skepticism and cynicism. True CXOs are void of pretense and are honest to themselves and others. A CXO is free to focus on being their best self because they allow themselves to be who God created them to be.

I interviewed for a promotion once where the vice president who I was interviewing with asked me how I would act differently if I were to get the position—to distinguish myself as a member of management. I stammered and stuttered for a few seconds in dismay from the question. Finally, I said I wouldn't do anything differently. I have always taken pride in being the same person at work as I am at home or out in a social setting. This wasn't a trick question, and she didn't like my response. As an inauthentic person herself, she believed I would need to show my co-workers (who I had already been working with for years) a different side of me if I were to get promoted to management. Thankfully, I didn't get offered that promotion.

Society is so heavily based on comparison and judgment it is hard to be authentic. People feel pressured to keep up with what everyone else is doing—as viewed on social media. We might under-report our weight a little on our driver's license, inflate our travel when will completing a mileage reimbursement form, or buy a house bigger than our salary allows to impress our friends. It is not until we can accept ourselves that others will accept us for who we are. The more comfortable you are with yourself the more comfortable others will be around you.

Vulnerability

Let me start by saying that being vulnerable is not a weakness. Let me repeat myself especially for the men; vulnerability is not a bad thing! To be vulnerable means to have emotional exposure and to embrace uncertainty. Christians are challenged to grasp onto the mystery that is our Faith; and the ambiguity transcends meaning and is what allows us to feel part of something bigger than ourselves. That requires vulnerability. So does a relationship; being a CXO requires us to be vulnerable enough to let people into our hearts.

I remember a few years back I had a kidney stone; my first and hopefully only. It came on like a speeding train and was the most debilitating pain I had ever experienced. I had been at work at the time, and as the discomfort grew throughout the morning I realized I needed to go see my doctor. That was a big admission. Like many men I can be stubborn about going to the doctor. The pain felt so intrusive I couldn't drive myself. It was not typical for me to reveal such complete and utter helplessness; I liked to do things for myself. God's grace gave me the chance to be vulnerable while I moaned and groaned in pain as my boss drove me to the clinic. I worked about thirty minutes from the doctor's office so my boss drove me in my car so I wouldn't need to pick it up later. This is another level of vulnerability; letting someone else drive my car. I have had a strong affinity for cars since childhood (something else I got from my dad) and wouldn't typically freely offer to let someone drive my car. Another co-worker followed us in her car to drive my boss back to the office. I was insistent that no one needed to stay with me at the clinic until my wife arrived.

While in the exam room, I had a chance to exercise more of my vulnerability muscles as the doctor and nurse laughed at me. Apparently my level of pain was so bad that I was squirming and flailing about pathetically; the kind of pain that when you see someone else in it, you can't help but to laugh. Lastly, I'll jump ahead to the point in the story when nurse Bob needed to give me a shot of morphine in my rear section for the pain. He came into the exam room and said, "I have good news and bad news. The good news is pain relief is on the way. The bad news is you have to get it in the butt." By this point I was so vulnerable and in so much pain I had my pants down before he even finished asking.

My relationships with my manager and co-worker strengthened because of the event. My appreciation of the value of vulnerability increased. We worked better together from that point on; we knew we had each other's backs and maintained loyalty. We had an emotional grasp of one another that proved beneficial many times over the years.

Hopefully you can learn the merit of being vulnerable without having to go through the type of pain a kidney stone brings. Take baby steps; you need not reveal all your deepest feelings or put yourself in a position to be taken advantage of. Start by acknowledging you do not have all of the answers, that you are open to having your mind changed, and that you aren't perfect.

Humility

As CXO we need to be open to having our opinions changed and accepting that we are not always right. You cannot do that if you are not humble.

Temperance is a virtue, and it takes self-restraint to fight against the temptation of our over exposed digital world we live in. It is hard to be humble when we are posting pictures and comments on social media all day. We live in a selfie world. To be humble is to remember it is not all about you. For a CXO to listen to others and sacrifice time and energy for others he or she needs to have humility. Faux CXOs spend all their time talking rather than listening and expect others to do things for them. CXOs strive to be the driving factor in the merit of someone else's human experience because it is holy and good, not to attain glory and accolades.

In his homily during a recent advent season, my church's pastor used the phrase, "Have a panoramic heart in a selfie world." He did so to describe the love we should strive for in our waiting for the coming of Jesus, and Christmas, at a time that has gotten so commercialized and self-absorbed. I thought the phrase was beautiful and spoke to the genius of humility; "A panoramic heart in a selfie world." I saw my pastor a couple days later and told him how much that phrase had stuck with me and I had been repeating it over and over in my head. I asked him if he came up with that himself or if he had heard it somewhere. He could have taken credit for it, but in his naturally humble style he admitted that one of his staff had come up with it. The next time I saw that staff member I told him how much I liked the phrase and he carried forward the example of humility by saying it wasn't to his credit; he said, "Sometimes things come to me as a gift from the Holy Spirit to make me sound smarter than I really am." I already told him I liked the catchphrase, he didn't need say how impressive it had been—and he didn't.

I used to golf with a gentleman who I worked with. Overall, he is a nice man, and I enjoyed his company. He is a superb golfer and fun to watch. I am just an okay golfer. The problem I had when golfing with him was he would tell you how good he was. If he hit a good shot, and I acknowledged it by saying something like, "Good shot Patrick," he would respond by saying, "Yah that was a good shot." And he was dead serious! He would describe to you what made it a good shot based on the wind conditions or architecture of the hole.

Over the years I developed a visceral, intransigent aversion to arrogance. I get immediately turned off by co-workers or friends who lead with their ego rather than their heart. My favorite scripture lesson on humility is the parable of the guests.

> He told a parable to those who had been
> invited, noticing how they were choosing the

places of honor at the table. "When you are invited by someone to a wedding banquet, do not recline at table in the place of honor. A more distinguished guest than you may have been invited by him, and the host who invited both of you may approach you and say, 'Give your place to this man,' and then you would proceed with embarrassment to take the lowest place. Rather, when you are invited, go and take the lowest place so that when the host comes to you he may say, 'My friend, move up to a higher position.' Then you will enjoy the esteem of your companions at the table. For everyone who exalts himself will be humbled, but the one who humbles himself will be exalted." (Luke 4:7-11)

I always operate as though I should recline at the lowest place. And my sense of humor is self-deprecating. It doesn't mean that I have a poor self-image or don't advocate for what is best for me. As CXO I am mature and emotionally independent in measuring my self-worth. I try to put others first and it has served me well.

Generosity

CXOs are kindhearted and boundless. They openly give of their time, talent, and treasure. A faux CXO will say "I don't have time for that." A true CXO will say, "I will make time to get that done." If you think you share, share more. If you believe you serve others, serve more. If you love, love more.

A few years ago my wife took my kids and me to a local housing complex for seniors and individuals with disabilities on a fixed income. It was the Christmas season, and we brought all the requisite supplies to make gingerbread houses. After we were done making the candy-covered dwellings and feeling proud, one resident came up to us and thanked us for doing the project. She said she now had a Christmas gift to give to her grandson—the decorated gingerbread house. If not for this activity he would have gotten nothing. Looking back on it, I alleged what we were doing was kind and generous; had I known the magnitude of the situation for many of these residents we could have been so much more generous. And for my own kids, who have gotten used to getting spectacular gifts from their grandparents, it was a healthy reminder of how fortunate they were. We decided to go deeper, and about six weeks later we brought all of the food to cook and serve a free lunch for the residents.

Your time, energy, talents, money, and resources are not yours to own or yours alone. They are gifts from God and are meant to be shared. Each day, we are called to bring and use all our gifts. I like to quantify it and suppose there were a number attached to it. Say I bring seven gifts to the table; I should put all seven to use each day. I need not concern myself that the person on my right has eleven gifts or the person on my left has one. I only desire for the person on my right to use all eleven of her gifts, and the person on my left to use his one, and that I use all seven of mine.

There you have it; six behaviors, attitudes, and skills that all end in "ity." They indicate what it means to be a CXO. I call them the "six little itys" and you can remember them by the image at the end of this chapter.

Chapter 6 Reflection Questions

1. Which of the "itys" are you most confident in?
2. Which of the "itys" do you need the most improvement in?

3. How, in your life, has vulnerability been a strength rather than a weakness? And how did that experience change you?

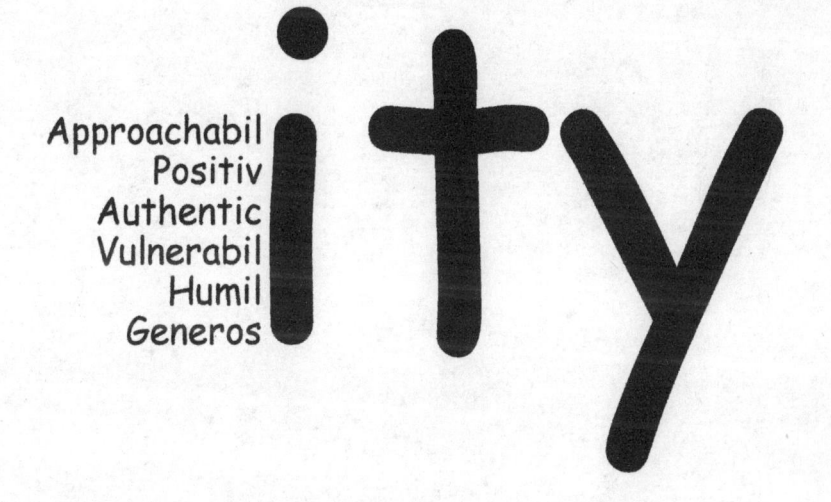

Approachabil
Positiv
Authentic
Vulnerabil
Humil
Generos
ity

7
WILL IT HURT?

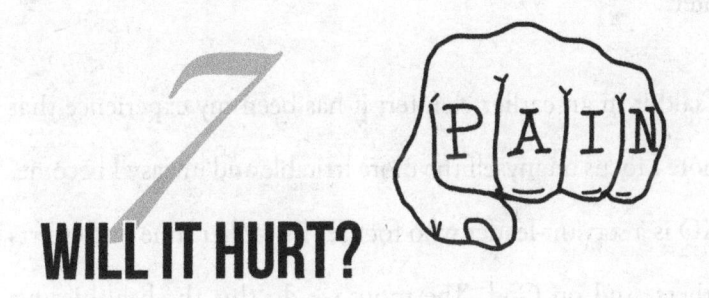

> I consider that the sufferings of this present time
> are as nothing compared with the glory to be
> revealed for us. Romans 8:18

Intentionally bringing more purpose and meaning to your life by working as a CXO has its effect on you; you can expect to be impacted in your heart, mind, body, and soul. Let's review the physical and sensory demands required of the position. And yes, this should be read tongue-in-cheek.

PHYSICAL AND SENSORY DEMANDS

Must be able to withstand extended periods of peace and joy. Occasional light lifting of arms to give hugs and pats on the back. Exposure to slight cheek pain due to prolonged smiling and laughter.

I said it in an earlier chapter; it has been my experience that the more I focus on myself the more irritable and uneasy I become. A CXO is a servant-leader who focuses his or her time and efforts on others, and on God. The more we do this the healthier we become; the more joyful we become. The more you do it the more conditioned you become; just like an athlete training his or her body. I lightheartedly mention hugs under physical demands, and truth be told I have grown in that area. In the past, I reserved hugs for close family. Today, I have come to appreciate the value of giving and receiving a hug between friends or co-workers. That growth sprouted from the competency of vulnerability and the principal duty of showing others that I appreciate them.

What you focus on expands. If you want more joy in life then focus on being joyful. If you want better friendships focus on being a better friend. If you are pessimistic and negative, then more negativity will come to you. Being a CXO is a force multiplier that can affect the whole person. You will see an increase in your effectiveness, your performance, your relationships, your faith, and your overall happiness.

Chapter 7 Reflection Questions

1. What area(s) of your life would benefit from a force multiplier?
2. Of the area(s) identified in question 1, what can you focus on to perpetuate more of the same?

WHAT ARE YOU WAITING FOR?

> Draw near to God, and he will draw near to you. Cleanse your hands, you sinners, and purify your hearts, you of two minds. James 4:8

You never know when or where you might encounter a CXO. I heard a story on the radio not too long ago about a guy, a truck driver, who knew what it meant to be a CXO. Whenever he would answer his cell phone while on the road and it would be a wrong number he would do something wonderful before ending the call. He would say, "Is there anything you need me to pray for? I am not crazy, I am a Christian, and I am wondering if there is anything you need me to pray for—for you?" Think about that. A stranger and a happenstance conversation, and they offer to pray for you. I am confident that gentleman was the driving force in determining the value of the experience for those strangers who inadvertently called the wrong number. He described the response from the callers as transformational—invariably people would talk with him and share struggles from their life that needed prayer.

Just like the truck driver, there are immediate openings for millions of CXO positions around the world. They come from all walks of life. And you can start today! God makes the platform available to you for you to take advantage of if you are alert and attentive. At the time I am writing this, we are experiencing civil discord, intolerance, and division around the globe. We can talk about the problems or how disgusted we are with how others act, or we can start the forward momentum. The world needs more CXOs. In the end, we will not be judged on whether we were right, won, or had the loudest voice. We will be judged on whether we loved.

Do not let past failures get in the way. Don't allow the fear that being a CXO is daunting or unrealistic prohibit you from beginning. The grace of God allows you to start anytime regardless of your past. In fact, there isn't even an application or interview process.

Mother Teresa, now Saint Teresa of Calcutta, once said, "God has not called me to be successful. He called me to be faithful." Consider being a CXO as a process and not an end point. You are better for engaging in the process even if not fully or permanently a CXO. You can't get fired from this position. You get a second, third, and "seven times seven" chance to be a CXO. Start today!

Saying yes to being a CXO will take sacrifice as most anything worthwhile does. For everything you say "yes" to there are dozens of other things you are saying "no" to. Accepting a CXO position means you say "no" to hatred, egoism, self-pity, gossiping, name calling, and many other destructors. I think you'll find it is well worth answering the call.

The world needs more CXOs; people who show it matters how you treat people. The reality is that you are creating experiences with people either way whether you know it or not; why not be intentional about it and create positive experiences? Start small, maybe with a "hello" to a stranger in the grocery store. Build on that and extend empathy to your boss or forgiveness to a family member who challenges you the most. Call a friend you haven't talked to in a while. Before long it will become easier and less scripted.

Take ownership over your actions and over your life. You are called to be the best you can be. Living a life of purpose and meaning will contribute to your mental and emotional health because you will feel as part of something bigger than you. Make connections; now is the time, today is the day. I wish you great luck and timeless energy to carry out the duties of a Chief Experience Officer faithfully.

It is not becoming of a CXO to be cynical and skeptical, but (or should I say "and") I am a realist. In my experience with adult learners, I find that we can be too quick to say, "This is great, but what about the other guy?" We tell ourselves we are doing fine and feel pity for the friends, family, and co-workers who aren't as advanced as we are. So if you are thinking this CXO business is fine in theory, but it won't matter if others aren't doing it, then I want to address that.

First, let me stress we are not perfect. There is always room to improve. Many learners prohibit the transfer of learning because they think they have already reached the desired outcome. I encourage you to be honest with yourself; there is no benefit to fooling yourself into believing you are a CXO when you are more often a faux CXO. Take an honest and earnest look in the mirror.

Second, God has graced us all with free will. We can choose our own path regardless of what others are doing. In fact, we might be the change needed to give a new perspective to someone else. CXOs are leaders who set the example. CXOs do not let others' unwillingness to strive to be better people deter us from wanting to be a better person. CXOs realize that we cannot expect others to change when we do not change ourselves.

One summer my family and I had been visiting relatives at their lake house in northern Wisconsin. I awoke one warm summer morning extra early before anyone else. I walked to the end of the pier and looked over the lake. It was like a perfect sheet of glass. Not a single imperfection anywhere and I could see clear across to the other side. I had been feeling extra hot and sticky, and with the smell of the previous night's campfire still on my body. I jumped in to cool off. As luck would have it, I was in the water for only a few seconds and got back out because I felt too cold. As I stood at the end of the pier, dripping wet, looking out over the lake, I watched the ripples I created reach all the way to the other side. I was in complete wonderment seeing the impact I made on the entire lake. How is it possible little old me, one jump, seven seconds in the water, and the effects were seen across the lake? We all have that power inside us. Change starts within. Then, and only then, can you expect to influence change in your friends, family, team, church, and community. There is no harm is trying.

Chapter 8 Reflection Questions

1. What do you anticipate being the biggest obstacles getting in the way of being a CXO?
2. Who can you turn to when you need help during the hard times?
3. What are some examples of things you need to say "no" to because you have a bigger "yes" burning inside you?

APPENDIX

> Keep repeating them to your children. Recite them when you are at home and when you are away, when you lie down and when you get up. Bind them on your arm as a sign and let them be as a pendant on your forehead. Write them on the doorposts of your houses and on your gates. Deuteronomy 6:7-9

DETERMINE.DESCRIBE.DRIVE

As mentioned in chapter two, a CXO reports to his or her values. Our personal set of core values guides our daily lives. Our values are our root system keeping us standing tall when life's strongest winds blow. If you don't have a defined set of values, I recommend you use the three-step process I have outlined for you. If you already possess a prescribed list of personal core values, you can skip ahead to step two for ideas on how to leverage them.

Step 1: Determine what your values are

I recommend a basic brainstorm. You could assemble your family and make it a group decision to have a core set of family values. Or, look at a pre-made list and select what most resonates with you. Examples of values are words like integrity, compassion, achievement, love, respect, humor, and courage. A simple online search will yield dozens of examples. I appreciate the website www.Values.com where you can find a list of sample values to select from, and many other valuable resources.

The key is, narrow it down to the top three-to-five values that are most important to you. Start with your top ten and then prioritize down from there. Keep in mind you are not saying that the other values are bad; just not the most important to you being the best you.

Personally, we have family values at our house. They are: Respect, Love, Gratitude, and Try Your Best. My wife, two children, and I selected them together using a simple voting method. We brainstormed an initial list of about ten and then each of us got to pick our top three. That got us to a majority result of four.

Some people make the mistake of not selecting specific values, and just saying that all values are important. In other words, I will try to live by them all. This is not practical. Here is the universal truth—if you don't commit to the one, you end up doing none. Selecting the top three-to-five values doesn't mean the other values are unimportant, less valuable, or that you don't practice them. It means when you need to fall back on something secure and comfortable when times get tense you will have a clearly defined set of principles to guide your way. Commit to a manageable number and you will be able to live by them.

Let me share an example to show my point. My wife is a teacher and, as such, when our kids were younger they were subjected to doing math flash cards in the summer to keep their skills sharp. As any siblings would be, mine are competitive with one another. On one occasion they decided to race and see who could get through their deck of flashcards the fastest, with mom as judge. My son had been working on division and my younger daughter had just started multiplication. However, before this competition was set to begin, my daughter went to her bedroom and got her addition deck of flash cards. Why is that? Because they were something comfortable she could fall back on when things got tense and something was on the line. She knew she could be successful with it and increase the likelihood of beating her brother. Your values can give you that same comfort level.

Step 2: Describe what they look like in day-to-day behavior

The next step is to designate what those values look like in day-to-day life. Each of your selected values should be given a definition and a description. For example, the value "integrity" can be defined as keeping your promises. And "integrity" could be described as taking out the garbage when you say you will do it.

Do not use another source's definition. These need to be your personal definitions and descriptions because every person or family will have their own interpretation. You, and your family if you have chosen a set of core family values, need to know what your values look like in day-to-day behavior.

I mentioned one of my family values is "Try Your Best." We talk about that a lot with our children regarding their involvement in extracurricular activities and their studies in school. If one of my children comes home lamenting over a bad grade on a test, the first question I ask is, "Did you try your best?" If they can honestly answer in the affirmative, then we can all rest easy with the result. I try to never correct my kids for making a physical mistake; however, we have had many conversations when I've noticed a lack of effort.

Step 3: Drive values awareness

Values clarification and alignment is not a "flavor of the day" proposition. You, and your family if you selected family values, will need regular re-enforcement of the values.

At my house, we hung the list of our values on the refrigerator. We talk about them frequently when faced with tough decisions. We are a work in progress; we don't always make the right choices. However, I am confident we all know what our family's values are—that is a beginning.

The following is a list of ideas of ways to drive your values awareness.

- Make your values part of the regular language of your conversations.

- Talk about your childhood to illustrate what is important to you and how it developed.
- Think about who you admire (real life or characters) and which of your values they are demonstrating.
- Reflect on examples from your life experiences that helped shape your values.
- Model the values to others.
- Focus on a value of the week or month and take a deeper dive into focusing on that value during prayer and meditation.
- Celebrate when you have success and recognize family members who demonstrate the values.
- Take advantage of teachable moments to talk about values.
- Post your values somewhere in the house.
- Talk about your values with others.
- Review your values daily as part of your prayer routine.
- Create consonance between your values and the types of activities you participate in and the work you do.
- Have consequences when values are not demonstrated.
- Listen to recordings and/ or read inspirational literature that reaffirms your values.

ABOUT THE AUTHOR

Photo: Fran Balistrieri, Madly Deeply Photography

A new author and masterful facilitator, Dan holds a degree in education and has over 20 years of experience in workplace learning and performance. He has worked at large for-profit and non-profit organizations. Dan has been blessed with the opportunity to conduct workshops on family, faith, leadership, educator, and professional development for many local organizations. He also serves as a catechist where he lives in southeastern Wisconsin. Dan is married and has two children.